Nancy Butterworth,

WHO ARE CHRISTIANS?

A Discourse,

DELIVERED IN MUSIC HALL, BOSTON, MASS.,

BY

WILLIAM DENTON.

BOSTON:
PUBLISHED BY WILLIAM DENTON.
FOR SALE BY WILLIAM WHITE AND COMPANY,
158 WASHINGTON STREET.

WHO ARE CHRISTIANS?

If Christianity, as taught in our evangelical churches, is true, the most important question that one man can ask another is, Are you a Christian? Next to this in importance must be the question, What constitutes a Christian?

Noah Webster says that a Christian is one who believes in Christ, and "especially one whose inward and outward life is conformed to the doctrines of Christ." According to this, there are two classes of Christians, — a general class who believe, and a special class who believe, and whose life accords with, the doctrines or teachings of Jesus. To the first class belong, probably, three-fourths of all the people of Christian countries, — England, France, Germany, Spain, Italy, indeed, of Europe generally, and the United States. They regard Jesus as the Messiah, the sent of God, the Christ, and think that salvation can only come by him. They are Christians, as Turks are Mohammedans.

Christians, then, fill our prisons, almshouses, lunatic-asylums, and houses of prostitution. Our thieves are Christian thieves, and our murderers Christian murderers. How rare it is for infidels to be convicted of theft, or hung for murder! On the gallows it is the name of Jesus the Christ that gives consolation to the dying criminal; and he expects, with the repentant thief, to be with him in Paradise. The late riots in New York were Christian riots. Our rowdies swear Christian oaths; and, when the death-angel appears to call them, they send for a Christian priest to prepare them for their departure.

Constantine the Great was a Christian,—he who murdered his son Crispus and his nephew Licinus, and suffocated his wife Faustus in a bath: he may be regarded, indeed, as the founder of our present Christian sabbath. Theodosius I., another Roman emperor, who murdered in cold blood seven thousand of the inhabitants of Thessalonica, without distinction of age, was a zealous and orthodox Christian; and so was Leo III., who commanded every person in his dominions to be baptized, under pain of banishment, and sentenced those to death who relapsed into idolatry after the ceremony.

Those men of Alexandria who murdered Hypatia were Christians to a man. Though she gave public lectures on philosophy, and proved herself to be one of the most noble women of her time, yet the Christian monks and rowdies, headed by a Christian priest, seized her in the street, dragged her into a Christian Church, stripped her naked, whipped her, cut her in pieces, and burned her mangled remains in the market-place.

Peter the Hermit was a famous Christian: clad in rags, and bare-footed, he wandered up and down

Europe, stirring up his fellow-Christians to rescue the Holy Land from the hands of the infidel Turks. Millions rallied to his call. "Their track," says Draper, "was marked by robbery, bloodshed, and fire." When they captured Jerusalem, "the brains of young children were dashed out against the walls; infants were pitched over the battlements; every woman that could be seized was violated; men were roasted at fires; some ripped up to see if they had swallowed gold. The Jews were driven into their synagogues, and burned; and nearly seventy thousand persons were massacred."

Father Dominic, who founded the Spanish Inquisition, was a Christian; and so were the wretches who applied its tortures. Torquemada, during his tenure of office as inquisitor-general, burned thousands, most of them fellow-Christians, who differed from him on some unimportant trifles. In less than three hundred years, the Spanish and Christian Inquisition burned alive more than thirty thousand persons, and condemned to various terms of imprisonment nearly three hundred thousand.

The Massacre of St. Bartholomew, in which sixty-six thousand persons were murdered for daring to be Protestants, was performed by Christians. In Rome, the papal Christians fired cannon and kindled bonfires, and Pope Gregory assisted at the celebration of a solemn mass, as a thanksgiving to God for his help in butchering their fellow-Christians. Indeed, to-day Christian Germans and Christian French are fighting; and the victories are duly celebrated by thanks to the Christian's God in the name of Jesus, the object of the Christian's faith.

"I deny that these were Christians," says one. "Think of Christian thieves, murderers, and prostitutes! Why, the statement is its own sufficient refutation." — "Who, then, are Christians?" I inquire. "Those only who obey the doctrines of Christ, and live the life of which he set a perfect example." This must be the second class of Christians to whom Webster refers. Where are we to find the doctrines of Jesus? In the New Testament, and especially in the Gospels, which are supposed to contain the commands that he gave in the very words in which they were uttered, infallibly reported by the inspired evangelists. Let us examine these, and compare them with the conduct of those who claim the Christian name, that we may discover who are the genuine Christians, and separate them from the miserable pretenders whom we have been considering.

Commencing with Matthew, who gives us a report of a famous sermon by Jesus himself, we find one of his commands to be, "Swear not at all . . . let your communication be, Yea, yea; Nay, nay: for whatsoever is more than these cometh of evil" (Matt. v. 34). And James, one of his disciples, who is supposed to have heard the discourse, reiterates the command, and even strengthens it: "Above all things, my brethren, swear not, neither by heaven, neither by the earth, neither by any other oath: but let your yea be yea; and your nay nay; lest ye fall into condemnation" (James v. 12). "Above all things," — above lying, then, above stealing, drunkenness, and even murder; and he who swears must, according to this, be the most guilty of all criminals.

Now, walk into one of our courts of justice. Hear what the judge says to a number of men who stand before him: "You solemnly swear, in the presence of Almighty God, that you will speak the truth, the whole truth, and nothing but the truth: so help you God." And the men hold up their right hands, and swear. Who can those men be? Are they Mohammedans, or ignorant pagans? One is a Catholic, another a Methodist, a third a Presbyterian, and all professing Christians; and there are none out of the millions professing the Christian name who regard these commands, except a handful of Quakers and Moravians. Can we consider those men Christians of the second class, who so grossly neglect such a plain and positive command of Christ as this?

In the same sermon, Jesus said, "Resist not evil; but whosoever shall smite thee on thy right cheek, turn to him the other also. And if any man will sue thee at the law, and take away thy coat, let him have thy cloak also. And whosoever shall compel thee to go a mile, go with him twain" (Matt. v. 39–41). In a report by Luke of the same discourse, we have these commands in a still stronger form: "Unto him that smiteth thee on the one cheek, offer also the other; and him that taketh away thy cloak forbid not to take thy coat also" (Luke vi. 29). Again he says, "Love your enemies; do good to them which hate you." These commands are plain; their meaning is evident: but who obeys them? Not the policeman who knocks down the man that strikes him, and takes him off to jail. Not the member of a Christian church who employs the policeman to resist the man whom he is unable or unwilling to resist himself. No policeman can be a true Christian: his business is to resist evil; and, when he ceases to do that, his work as a policeman is at an end. If a policeman could be a Christian, a man who lives by stealing could be an honest man. Our jailers, magistrates, judges, and attorneys, are constantly engaged in resisting evil, and even boast of what they accomplish in this way. They seem to have agreed to treat Jesus as we treat the insane, saying, Yes, yes, to all he utters, but never for a moment intending to obey his commands. From the decreasing ranks of our genuine Christians we must then take jailers, magistrates, judges, attorneys and justices: they not only disobey these commands of Jesus, but they live by their disobedience of them, and are constantly engaged in encouraging others to disobey them. Soldiers, from the man in the ranks to the general, must be counted out. They may plunder their enemies, shoot them, stab them; but, if they love them, they are spoiled for soldiers. What would a captain say to the man in his company who allowed the enemy to strike him, and never attempted to return the blow, but allowed him to strike the second time, and still made no resistance? A Christian soldier would be more useless than an idiotic school-teacher; and a musket is as much out of place in a Christian's hands as a telescope is at the eye of a blind man.

But the whole frame-work of our government rests on the soldier. Disobey the law, and the constable serves a warrant on you; resist the constable, and the general police are called out, or special constables sworn in; successfully resist these, and the State militia are employed; and if they should be too feeble to overcome the resistance, then the soldiers employed by the general government become the last resort: if they fail, the government is gone, and the successful resisters establish theirs in its place. Since soldiers cannot be Christians, all government officers who hold their situations by the soldiers' resistance share in their guilt, and must be counted unworthy of the Christian name.

But Christians everywhere act as if these commands of Jesus had never been given, or, being given, that they mean the very contrary of what they say. Joseph Smith, the Mormon prophet, was once asked what he thought of that passage of Scripture which says, "Whosoever shall smite thee on thy right cheek, turn to him the other also." — "Ah!" said Joseph, "Jesus Christ was a smart man, the wisest of men: he knew that a man might hit you accidentally or playfully, and, before resisting it, he wished you to make sure that he was in earnest, and that he meant you, by turning to him the other; but, if he hits you then, go into him like a thousand of brick." By the way that Christians generally act, one might suppose that they held a similar opinion with regard to its meaning.

Again Jesus says, "When thou prayest, enter into thy closet; and, when thou hast shut thy door, pray to thy Father which is in secret." Some Christians' praying is doubtless done after this fashion; but a large proportion of it is done in a very different way. Christian closets are very large in these days, and are generally furnished with steeples. The pompous clergyman in his sable robe, prayer-book before him, in stereotyped phrases offers his supplications in the presence of the assembled congregation. Another, before five hundred people, closes his eyes, lifts up his hands, and proceeds to inform God what he is, what he has done, and advise him for half an hour as to what he had better do. Not content with setting the commandments of Jesus at defiance themselves, these professed Christians establish meetings for public prayer, where men, and recently women, are encouraged to set the teachings of Jesus at defiance; and that is actually called a "Christian duty," which is in direct opposition to the teaching and practice of Jesus.

What sermon did he ever commence with a prayer? How many prayer-meetings did he establish or attend? Had he been like our modern Christians, we should have had some such record as this in the New Testament: "Now there was a prayer-meeting in Cana of Galilee, and Jesus and his disciples were there. Jesus opened the meeting by giving out one of the Psalms of David, and then called upon brother Simon Peter to pray, which he did in a voice of thunder, and with the unction of the Holy One: he was followed by brothers James and John, and all the disciples; and the power of the Lord was felt in their midst, so that the scribes and Pharisees marvelled, and a revival broke out, and many hundred souls were soundly converted to God." The difference between this and the statements made in the Gospels respecting the methods of Jesus represents the difference between Christianity and what passes for it at the present day. Had Jesus been like our present Christian ministers, he would have paid but little attention to men's bodies, he would have wasted but little time in curing their diseases: he would have established prayer-meetings, and formed societies from Nazareth to Jericho, and got up camp-meetings on the shores of Gennesaret, where he and his disciples would have prayed, and preached damnation to all unrepenting sinners, and salvation to all who should believe on a to-be-crucified Redeemer.

In the famous Sermon on the Mount, Jesus also says, "Give to him that asketh of thee, and from him that would borrow of thee turn not thou away" (Matt. v. 42). Luke's report also adds, "Of him that taketh away thy goods, ask them not again;" for, he says, "if ye lend to them of whom ye hope to receive, what thank have ye? for sinners also lend to sinners, to receive as much again. But love your enemies, and do good, and lend, hoping for nothing again, and your reward shall be great" (Luke vi. 30–34). This is also very plain: the disciples of Jesus are to be as widely different from sinners, and as easily distinguished, as sheep are from goats. But is this the case? Where are the men or women who obey these commands, or even try to obey them? It would only be necessary for the beggars to stand at the doors of our churches, to render themselves independently rich in a twelvemonth, if the professed Christians who worship in them were obedient to the commands of their Master. Where are the Christians, if those only are such who obey these commands? Are there any among the brokers of Wall Street or State Street? How many can Beacon Street show, or even Washington or Tremont Streets? It would require something brighter than Diogenes' lantern to find them. How do Christians lend? I find they are not averse to six per cent; nor do they often object to eight, even when the usury laws forbid it. Nor will they lend then without the best of security. They do not consider two per cent a month extravagant, if a man's necessities compel him to pay it; and they have no compunctions of conscience when they foreclose a mortgage, turn a man's family out, and take from them a five-thousand-dollar house on which they had lent but five hundred. A poor Christian wants to save his home from the clutches of some legal freebooter. Will his brother Christian lend him the money without interest, even if he has a million, and could do it as well as not? So seldom is it done, that such cases are almost unknown.

Had these commands of Jesus been the very opposite of what they are, the conduct of professing Christians would be almost in exact harmony with them. "Give nothing to him that asketh of thee, and from him that would borrow of thee turn thou away." "If any man take away thy goods, place him where there will be no opportunity to do it again." "Lend only to those of whom ye hope to receive, and where principal and interest are secured, then your reward shall be great." Read the passages thus, and I will find you obedient disciples in every church of the land.

I read also in this mountain sermon, "Lay not up for yourselves treasures upon earth, where moth and rust doth corrupt, and where thieves break through and steal." How many Christians obey this command? Few besides those who are so poor that they have nothing to lay up. If those only are Christians who obey the teachings of Jesus, all depositors in banks must be counted out, all holders of stocks and bonds. No free-mason can be a Christian, no odd-fellow, or son of temperance. All these have laid up for themselves treasures on earth, and have thereby forfeited all right to the treasures of heaven.

"*But Jesus never meant what you suppose.*" Who informed thee that Jesus did not mean what he said? Dost thou know better how to embody his meaning in words than He whom thou believest to be Lord of all the earth? It is passing strange, if he did not mean what he said, that he did not say what he meant.

"*But to obey such commands would make all Christians poor.*" Certainly; and this is just what is needed: Jesus evidently intended his disciples to be poor, and very poor. Nothing shows more clearly how the Christian standard has been lowered than the fact that rich men frequently claim to be Christians. The very first sentence that Jesus uttered in his Sermon on the Mount, according to Luke, was, "Blessed be ye poor; for yours is the kingdom of God." "Wha!" I hear some poverty-stricken wretch say, "is there any such passage as that in the Bible? Did the dear Jesus say that we the poor are blessed, and that ours is the kingdom of God?" I don't wonder that you ask the question. It is one of those passages that no minister chooses for a text, and that one never hears quoted from the pulpit; but here it is (Luke vi. 20): "Blessed be ye poor,"—p-o-o-r, poor. More than that, he says, "Woe unto you that are rich, for ye have received your consolation" (Luke vi. 24). He declares that "it is easier for a camel to go through the eye of a needle than for a rich man to enter into the kingdom of God." Either the needle must be larger than needle ever was, or the camel smaller than camel ever can be ; or no rich man can be a Christian, if this statement of Jesus is correct. Of course, Christians must be poor; and Jesus, in insisting upon poverty, did the greatest service to mankind, if his fearful statements are true. I am here this afternoon to preach — what has never before been heard in Boston — the genuine gospel of Jesus ; not the emasculated gospel of the fashionable churches, but that of the homeless, bedless wanderer of Nazareth. You never heard it before, and never would hear it in any ecclesiastical edifice ; for they are built by the very men whom that gospel declares woe against, and for whom the fire of its hell is prepared.

Read the parable of the rich man and Lazarus (Luke xvi. 19) : "There was a certain rich man, which was clothed in purple and fine linen, and fared sumptuously every day." No intimation that he was either a drunkard, or licentious, dishonest, or even niggardly ; but he was rich. And there was a beggar laid at his gate, so poor that he desired to be fed with the crumbs that fell from the rich man's table. No intimation that he was conscientious, truthful, or even pious ; but he was poor, — one of those whose is the kingdom of God. The beggar died, and was carried by angels into Abraham's bosom : the rich man also died, and was buried ; but in hell he lifted up his eyes, being in torment ; nor could all his entreaties procure a drop of water to cool his parched tongue while tormented in the scorching flame. Here is the woe denounced upon the rich, here the terrible fate that awaits them. No wonder that James said, "Go to now, ye rich men, weep and howl for your miseries that shall come upon you." When the rich man in the parable asks Abraham that Lazarus may dip the tip of his finger in water and cool his tongue, the answer of Abraham is, "Son, remember that thou in thy lifetime receivedst thy good things, and likewise Lazarus evil things; but now he is comforted, and thou art tormented." The hungry are to rejoice, for by and by they will be fed; the mourners, for they will be comforted; and the miserably poor, for the joys of heaven await them. But this hell-tortured sinner, who might not have the slightest mitigation of his penalty, was guilty of the crime of being rich: he had had his good things, and now it is turn about; and in his fate all rich men may see the doom that awaits them: the smoke of their torment must ascend forever. Nor is it a donation of a hundred dollars to foreign missions that will save you, or two hundred to the Rev. Theophilus Hardshell's salary: your only chance for salvation is to become poor.

A young man comes running to Jesus: he is evidently in earnest, and says, "Good Master, what good thing shall I do, that I may have eternal life?" Suppose the answer of Jesus had never been recorded, and the professing Christians of the various sects had been left to fill in the answer, each according to his notion. "I have no doubt," says one, "that he told him there was nothing to do but to exercise saving faith in him as the Messiah." "He must have commanded him," says another, "to pray at least three times a day, to attend divine service every sabbath, and live a Christian life." "I can tell you just what he told the young man," a third would have confidentially exclaimed; "and that is, simply to believe in him as the Christ, and be immersed in his name." Very fortunately, the answer of Jesus has been recorded; and it is such a one as no member of the three hundred Christian sects would ever have supposed. He first tells him that he must keep the commandments; but this the young man declares he has done from his youth up: and then he asks the all-important question, "What lack I yet?" Now we shall have the very essence of Christianity: keeping the commandments was Jewish, and men had practised it for centuries before Jesus came. If Christianity is true, from the lips of the Master of life is about to fall the words that contain the key to bliss eternal. "Sell that thou hast, and give to the poor, and come and follow me." Imagine how chop-fallen the young man looked! How many young men who compose our Christian associations would have looked otherwise? Only those that had nothing to sell. "He went away sorrowful; for he had great possessions." Had Jesus tried the solid men of Boston, how many would have obeyed him? Not a soul. The difference between them and the young man would have been, that they would have gone away angry instead of sorrowful. If the Christian missionaries of to-day preached such a gospel as Jesus did, their disciples would be as few.

"*But Christianity does not require that a man should strip himself in that way.*" The sham Christianity of the churches does not; but the Christianity of Jesus does. His commands are, "Sell that ye have, and give alms" (Luke xii. 33). "Take no thought for your life, what ye shall eat, nor yet for your body, what ye shall put on." "Take no thought for the morrow" (Matt. vi. 25, 34). Jesus and his disciples wandered about Galilee, sleeping on the ground or in a fishing-boat, knowing not to-day how to-morrow's dinner would be obtained. Jesus appears to have been as regardless of to-morrow as the birds, whose practice he recommends. The members of the earliest Christian Church appear to have understood the commands of Jesus literally, and they acted accordingly. They sold their possessions, and laid the money at the apostles' feet; and distribution was made to every one according to his need (Acts ii. 45).

Let men obey the teachings of Jesus, and how long would they be rich, or have possessions? Let the strongest bank in Boston put out a sign, "Here we lend, hoping for nothing in return; we give to all who ask of us, and of those who take our goods we ask them not again." Though the parties were rich as the Rothschilds in the morning, and as sure of hell as Dives, they would be stripped as bare as Lazarus before night, and be just as certain of a place in Abraham's capacious bosom.

Where is the church that demands of its members obedience to these vital Christian duties? Jesus says, "Believe in me." They do it, and are not at all backward in saying so. Christianity is now a fashionable religion; and nothing can be easier than to be a floating chip on the current of public opinion. Jesus says, "When ye pray, say, Our Father:" and this how ready all are to perform, from the Unitarians to the ranters, from the prattling babe to the gray-haired sinner of ninety; and ask for their daily bread as if the breakfast-loaf depended on their morning petition. This also costs nothing. Jesus says, handing the wine-cup to his disciples, "Do this, as oft as ye do it, in remembrance of me;" and, although there is no positive command, they are eager to attend to the slightest hint of their Master, and down goes the poisonous alcoholic compound as the mystical blood of Jesus. He also says, "He that believeth, and is baptized, shall be saved." "Then we must be baptized," say the Baptists. "Yes, our little ones," say the pedo-Baptists; and up come the little children in the arms of their parents, and are sprinkled in the name of the triune Jehovah; and down go the children of a larger growth in the arms of the priest, to be dipped in the same name. This also costs next to nothing, and is often a passport into what is called good society. But when Jesus says, "Lend, hoping for nothing again," "Give to him that asketh of thee," "Sell that ye have, and give alms," all are stone-deaf; or, if they hear, they are quite sure that he does not mean what he says. Jesus may beckon for them to tread the path that he has trod; but they are all blind. This costs something; this strips them and tries them; this tests their faith. Jesus is reported as saying, "When the Son of man cometh, shall he find faith on the earth?" and I think, if he should come now, he would find the pretending members of his church to be infidels to a man: there is no faith in Jesus in the land. Let millionnaires distribute what they have robbed from the poor, when they take the Christian name; let them sell their mansions to-day, and distribute to the necessitous, and know not where they shall lay their heads to-morrow; let those Christian ministers who denounce all who do not accept their standard of Christianity set the example by reducing themselves to abject poverty, and then we shall have evidence of their sincerity at least.

Who are genuine Christians? They cannot be those lords over God's heritage, who pocket from five to fifteen thousand dollars a year for preaching a gospel scarcely an item of which Jesus could recognize. They cannot be among those sleek church-goers who pay from a hundred to a thousand dollars a year for the privilege of sitting in a cushioned pew, and listening to Rev. Silver-Tongue as he proves how easy it is for a camel to go through a needle's eye. Boston, among its regiment of preachers, cannot find a single man; and the New-York and Brooklyn pounders, expounders, and ten-pounders, are not a whit more Christian than their Boston brethren. If the Christians only are sheep, they are left-hand goats, to a man; and the Judge's fatal "Depart!" must ring through their guilty souls in "the last great day." Nor are the members of our so-called Christian churches in a much more hopeful condition. Not only is it impossible to find a man who obeys the commands of Jesus, we cannot even find one who tries to obey them; and, if we did, his Christian brethren would be among the first to conclude that he had taken leave of his senses.

If any of you still think that you are Christians, and that, on account of this, Jesus will save you from the curses pronounced on the disobedient, let me refer you to the sixteenth chapter of Mark. I read, "He that believeth and is baptized shall be saved; but he that believeth not shall be damned." Now comes the question of questions: Are you a believer? for, if you are not, damnation is yours. Jesus himself gives the test by which you may decide: "These signs shall follow them that believe: in my name shall they cast out devils; they shall speak with new tongues; they shall take up serpents; and, if they drink any deadly thing, it shall not hurt them; they shall lay hands on the sick, and they shall recover." Can you cast out devils in the name of Jesus? Can you speak with new tongues? It may be difficult to tell when the devils are in, and perhaps still more to tell when they are out; it may be impossible for us to tell whether any peculiar speech that you may utter is a veritable language or not: but can you handle serpents with impunity, say rattlesnakes, vipers, or copperheads? Can you drink any deadly thing without injury? — a dose of arsenic, for instance, a few grains of corrosive sublimate, or half a pint of sulphuric-acid? Can a man be found among the millions professing the Christian name that would submit to the test, to say nothing about being unharmed afterward? Or can you lay your hands on the sick, and they recover? I hear of Spiritualists doing this at times; but where are the Christians that can do it? And yet it is evident, if Jesus states what is true, that those who cannot do these things will be damned. Out of the way, you shams! — you Roman Catholic, with your seven sacraments, your holy water, your Latin gabble, your fantastic dresses! Away with you, monks, priests, cardinals, and infatuated popes, and take your *Pater-Nosters* and *Ave-Marias*, your litanies and your solemn masses, with you! What are they good for? The whole pile of your mummery never made a single Christian, and cannot save from damnation one guilty soul. You need not come, Episcopalian, to take his place. What better is your prayer-book than his mass-book? Are your two sacraments any more efficacious than his seven? your damnatory creed any more soul-saving than his? You can make Episcopalians by the million; but there is not a Christian among them; and, if Jesus speaks what is true, they will every one be damned with the common herd. Here come the Presbyterians. "We are *the* Christians, orthodox, evangelical. We have thrown overboard unscriptural Popery, unchristian Episcopalianism; and we are the true followers of the Saviour." You, with your cloud-cleaving spires, your velvet-cushioned pews and your tasselled pulpits, your ten-thousand-dollar ministers and millionnaire members, — you Christians? Then are misers generous, drunkards temperate, and Hottentots the most beautiful of mankind. You need not crowd in, Methodist, Baptist, Quaker, Shaker, Unitarian, Universalist, and Adventist, — shams, every one. Jesus can only say to you all, "Depart from me: I never knew you!" You have built on the sand, and your structure must fall when the wrath of God is revealed on those who obey not the gospel of his Son.

If none are to be saved but Christians, where, my professing brother, will you appear?

I can see the last great day, "the day for which all other days were made." Down from heaven descends the Master, surrounded with the shining host; and at the sound of that trumpet whose call the very dead hear, up come earth's buried hosts. I behold all the Christians sects, marshalled by their leaders and under their respective banners, come before the throne of Him whose name had been their boast. The Roman Catholics, a myriad-membered throng, approach; and a venerable prelate stands as their mouthpiece before the "dread tribunal." "On what grounds do ye claim the Christian name, and a place in my kingdom?" said the once meek Nazarene, but now the lion of the tribe of Judah, with flaming vengeance in his eye and a dagger in every word. "Thou gavest to Peter the keys of the kingdom of heaven; and we have faithfully obeyed his successors, and proclaimed their decisions infallible. We have styled the holy Mary, thy mother, Mother of God, and given to her all but divine homage. We have built the most magnificent cathedrals, and drained from the poor more money for thy cause than any other people on earth. We have persecuted to death, wherever we have had the power, all who would not bow down to thy name, as our church directed: we burnt them at the stake, racked them on the wheel, hung them on the gibbet, and tortured them in all ways that our ingenuity could devise, to drive their heresies from them, and save precious souls. Surely we are thy people, and shall be allowed to enter into thy kingdom, and sit down with thee."

"Did you not know," and his voice sounded like thunder, "that Peter was he to whom I said, 'Get thee behind me, Satan!' and that he denied me with oaths and curses? What authority had you from me to call his pretended successors infallible? When I was on earth, my disciples wished to call down fire from heaven on those who rejected me; but I replied, as you know, 'The Son of man came not to destroy men's lives, but to save them.' Was it for you, then, in my name, to torture and burn men because they would not submit to a tyrannical church, — the most infernal that was ever established among men? My mother did no more than any other woman might have done in her place, and was no more divine than the mothers of my poor, whom you robbed to build your pompous piles, and feed your pampered church. Traitors to humanity, lovers of darkness, torturers of the conscientious, plunderers of the poor, depart from me!" Then the banners drooped, the proud prelates hung their heads, and the duped multitude blushed for shame as they moved on, and made room for the Presbyterians, who came boldly, in no degree disconcerted by the fate of the Romanists that had preceded them. "We are Christians," said they, "and we claim the kingdom which is ours by faith." — "What have ye done to deserve it?" said He on the throne. They answered, "We rescued thy Church and thy Word from the hands of the polluted wretches that preceded us, and uplifted thy banner, that had been trampled in the dust, and made it sacred in the eyes of the respectable in all Christian lands. We built the best of churches, paid millions for home and foreign missions, and made thy name to be honored by the rich and influential everywhere. We erected colleges for training young men to preach thy Word; and our doctors of divinity were renowned throughout the civilized world."

"Is this what I commanded you to do?" and his eye blazed like lightning; and a shudder ran through the multitude, so that they trembled, as he spoke, like a leaf on an aspen-tree. "You rescued my Church and my Bible? You never did either. My Church exists alone in the hearts of those who obey my instructions; and from whom did my Word need to be rescued more than from you who denied its meaning, and by every deed of your lives set at nought its requirements? You made my name honored by misrepresenting my character, and belying my gospel; and in my kingdom there is no place for such as you." And I saw the sad, solemn multitude depart like a funeral procession, to make room for the next claimants of the Christian's reward.

Confidently came a greater host, a host no man might number: a million columns filed before the throne, and they looked as if they might, in case of refusal, take heaven itself by storm. They were the Methodists. "We are thine," said they, "the children of the King; and we come to thee for our crown and our kingdom." —"Why should I give crowns to you? What proofs can you present of your relationship to me?" said the Judge. "Like thee we went among the poor and the lowly, we formed prayer-meetings, established class-meetings, got up revivals, and swept millions into thy Church and thy fold. We, too, have built churches in thy name; in thy name have founded colleges, and sent out preachers to the remotest bounds of the earth." — "I know you," said the Judge; and, as he said it, I saw darkness upon their faces like the shadow of a cloud on a mountain-side. "You went among the poor and lowly: ye did well; but did you go to distribute all that you had? Did you give to those who asked you? Did you lend, hoping for nothing? Did you denounce the tyrant lordlings who held my people in bondage, and wrung from them the fruits of their labor to pamper their pride? Who told you to form prayer-meetings and class-meetings? Who commanded you to get up revivals, build churches, and send preachers to declare a gospel which they preached, instead of my gospel, scarcely a word of which they ever uttered? My crowns are not for such as you, and my heaven cannot reward pretenders, or their dupes." And the weeping Methodists followed the Presbyterians and the Romanists, as all other Christian sects followed them; for in the heaven of Jesus the Christ there was no place found by them.

Where, then, shall we find the true Christians? I will give you the gospel-marks by which they may be distinguished; and, when you find one, you cannot be mistaken. They never swear, not even in a court of justice; they do not resist evil, and, if any man hits them on one cheek, they turn the other; they lend, hoping for nothing again; they give to all who ask of them; they sell what they have, and give alms; they take no thought for the morrow; they take no thought about what they shall eat, drink, or wear; they wash one another's feet. When they make a feast, they do not invite their friends nor their acquaintances nor their rich neighbors, but the poor, the halt, and the blind. They love their enemies; but they hate their fathers, mothers, sisters, brothers, husbands or wives, their children, and their own lives: for all these Jesus commanded. Should there be any doubt still remaining, you will know them by this: they can cast out devils, speak with new tongues, handle serpents, drink deadly poison with impunity, and heal the sick by laying their hands upon them. "But there are no such people," I think I hear you say. Certainly not; and hence there are no Christians in your sense, — none who obey the commands of Jesus; and indeed Jesus himself was no Christian, if this alone constitutes one. Like all other men, his ideal was different from his actual life. He says, "Whosoever calleth his brother a fool is in danger of hell-fire;" yet he repeatedly calls the Pharisees "fools and blind." He says, "Resist not evil," yet with a scourge drives the traffickers out of the temple, and overturns the tables of the money-changers. He tells men to be perfect, as their Father in heaven is perfect; and yet says there is but One good, that is God. He says, "Take no thought for the morrow." Hear him in the Garden of Gethsemane, as he prays, "O my Father, if it it be possible, let this cup pass from me." What cup? The cup of sorrow that he was to drink on the morrow. If none get to heaven but those who obey the commandments of Jesus, then Jesus himself will be absent: he too will be cast into outer darkness, where there is weeping, wailing, and teeth-gnashing. If Jesus was not a genuine Christian, what chance has any one else to be?

I do not, of course, blame any one for failing to be a

Christian. It is not in the power of humanity to be; and for men even to try to be would be most disastrous. It was this that made a eunuch of Origen, filled the Church with idle nuns and beggarly monks, and to-day makes celibates of hundreds of Shakers, who, but for their unfortunate faith, might be exemplary parents, and leave the world better than they found it. It has made multitudes fools for Christ's sake, who might have been intelligent and happy men and women. Let those who desire to become Christians give to those who ask of them, and lend, hoping for nothing again, and the list of paupers would soon be largely increased, and the idle and the industrious would be equally cursed. There is often no better way to cure a man of Christianity than to induce him to try to live his faith. These members of Christian churches, then,—these Christian ministers too, who "deal damnation round the land,"—are Christians in no other sense than the mass of believers in Jesus outside of the Church; and, if their Master is to be believed, their damnation is as certain as that of those they denounce. They are Christian ministers, as our thieves are Christian thieves; and the churches in which they preach are Christian churches, as our jails are Christian jails, and our drink-houses, Christian grog-shops. They have taken just as much of the doctrine of Jesus as they pleased, mixed it with a set of monstrous fables of their own, or of other pretended Christians, from Paul down; and, having baptized this as Christianity, they curse every one who will not bow down to the idol that they have set up.

There are multitudes of well-meaning people, who

have been educated in the Christian faith, or what goes by that name, who are sincerely desirous to obey the teachings of Jesus, because they believe it to be their duty. Many such are made unhappy by their inability to live the life that their faith demands. What a satisfaction it must be to know that there is not the least necessity for any one to be a Christian! our welfare in this life or the next does not in the slightest degree depend upon it. You can be a philosopher, as Humboldt was, and be no Christian, as he was none; you may be a poet, with Shelley; a philanthropist with Henry C. Wright, who had long cast off the Christian name and the Christian pretence; you can be a good father or mother, a good citizen, a lover of man, and a doer of right, a practiser of temperance and every virtue, and yet be no Christian. And a man may be a thief, drunkard, murderer, adulterer, hypocrite, and brute, and yet be a Christian in the only sense in which any man can be a Christian.

Think of the time, labor, and energy wasted in the attempt to make men Christians. Think of the thousands of missionaries roaming over the world, and spending their lives in converting men from one form of superstition to another. Think of the millions spent in Massachusetts to convert men to the dogmas of twenty contending sects, that are no more Christian than the Roman Church is catholic. Instead of Bible-classes, where our young people are taught what the Bible means, and often what it does not mean, let us have classes of physiology, phrenology, geology, and astronomy; schools for adults, in which grammar, elocution, music, and drawing will be taught, and where instruction can be obtained in the moral duties which grow out of our relations to each other and to nature. Then every member will learn something useful, not only for this life, but that will be capital with which to start in the next. Instead of Christians, let us have whole-souled, well-developed men and women, who will do right because right-doing is best for humanity. Instead of Christian ministers, let us have human ministers,—men bound by no creed, tied to no church, cursed by no Bible; men who will simply ask, What does Nature teach? and, having learned this, seek to impress the truth on the minds of their fellows.

BOOKS FOR THINKERS.

Our Planet: Its Past and Future;

OR,

LECTURES ON GEOLOGY.

By WILLIAM DENTON.

(Fourth Thousand.)

"The New-York Tribune" says of it, "This is a book for the masses, — a book that should be read by every intelligent man in the country."

"Mr. Denton has certainly succeeded better than any American author I know, in making a really interesting, readable book on Geology." — *Henry A. Ward, Professor of Geology in Rochester University.*

"A meritorious contribution to popular scientific literature." — *Scientific American.*

"Prof. Denton divests Geology of most of its technicalities, and makes it as interesting as a romance." — *Herald of Health.*

"A book which is hardly less than the *beau ideal* of a scientific treatise designed strictly for popular reading. It is interesting as a novel." — *Boston Commonwealth.*

Price, $1.50

THE SOUL OF THINGS;

OR,

Psychometric Researches and Discoveries.

(Fourth Edition.)

By WILLIAM AND ELIZABETH M. F. DENTON.

"We have here a marvellous book. It is calm, and seems perfectly sincere; and yet it makes larger drafts upon our credulity than any work we ever before met with. The old alchemists never conceived of any thing half so strange. Spiritualism, with all its wonders, is scarcely a vestibule to what we are introduced to here.

"Were there any reliance to be placed on these revelations, it would be impossible to estimate the value of this newly-discovered power. It would resolve a thousand doubts and difficulties, make geology as plain as day, and throw light on all the grave subjects that time has so effectually obscured." — *New-York Christian Ambassador.*

"In the varied wonders they describe, there is a peculiar and intense interest. If what is claimed in this book to be true, it records the most remarkable discovery yet made as regards the capacities of the human mind in its abnormal state." — *Norfolk-County Journal.*

"There is much extraordinary matter in these pages. It is a volume emphatically deserving of the reader's choicest study." — *Boston Traveller.*

"Though as concise as a text-book, we read 'The Soul of Things' with the fascination of a work of fiction. Indeed, it is truth itself, stranger than fiction, written in the vivid style which is a part of Mr. Denton's remarkable power." — *American Spiritualist.*

"The reader will be amazed to see the curious facts here combined in support of the theory of the DENTONS. The natural facts adduced are more than are dreamed of in much of our philosophy." — *Albany Standard and Statesman.*

Price $1.50.

www.ingramcontent.com/pod-product-compliance
Lightning Source LLC
LaVergne TN
LVHW020742120826
845150LV00010B/2345

* 9 7 8 1 4 1 8 1 9 4 4 9 9 *